Recipes &
From Israel

Volume One

DEBORAH S. COHEN

Bible quotations are taken from the New King James Version (NKJV), Copyright 1982 by Thomas Nelson, Inc. and the New International Version, Copyright 1973, 1978, 1984, 2011 by Biblica, Inc.

ISBN: 9798344631530

Printed in the USA

Photography: Deborah S. Cohen, Cherri Beard, Chris Maita

Cover Photo: Noam Cohen

Cartoons: Chris Maita

Editing: Teresa Sarros

Book Design: Cherri Beard

Publishing: Cherri Beard

For more information about the author,

Visit: www.declaringzioninternational.org

e-mail: declaringzionintl@yahoo.com

Rumble: DeclaringZionInternational

YouTube: Declaring Zion International

Facebook: Deborah N Noam Cohen

DEDICATION

My precious husband Noam has been the number one taste tester in our house in the Galilee, Israel. He has been supportive as I create recipes from the abundance that the Lord has given to this small strip of land called the Promised Land. Noam Ezra Cohen, you are the best of the best as you have endured my experiments with spices and adding special ingredients together.

My best friends in Israel have been the best taste testers and have shared their insights and gentle suggestions after so bravely tasting all that I have put before them. David and Sigal, thank you for your love and your ability to give suggestions in a loving manner to me. I can also add Leveu and Hyah, Mark and Sherol, Kfir and Sylvanna, Elon and Ofra, and Danny and Syhava, especially if I created something without dairy. Lorraine, Jennifer, and Sherwood, you were always so willing to taste all that I made and gave me such great suggestions! Oh, and how can I forget David from Sar El Tours who I truly believe loved everything I had him taste.

But most of all, I thank the Lord for giving me this ability to have fun in the kitchen and such courage to try all the fruits and vegetables and spices that I had never seen before or knew about! I am so thankful for all that He has surrounded me with in this amazing Land. He has given me such a love for His Covenant Land and people, and an appreciation for the abundance that He has given His people to enjoy.

Thank you, Lord, for my life!

RECIPES AND STORIES FROM ISRAEL

TABLE OF CONTENTS

Main Courses

Desserts

Deborah's Table Settings

INTRODUCTION

Let me begin by saying I am a wee bit dyslexic with numbers and words, so I must say with a smile on my face, "Enjoy, and make these recipes at your own risk!" My wonderful sisters, Terry, Cherri, and Chris were my kitchen testers on almost every recipe I created. We all laughed as I shared with them my adventures in creating recipes with the beautiful, bountiful products of the Promised Land. The joy of the Lord and the laughter between us is a memory I will never forget. They encouraged me to finish this cookbook because they loved the recipes and the stories I shared with them, and they wanted you to love them, too!

I am so blessed to live in Israel where, no matter where I am in the Land, I see orchards and fields full of the richness that the Lord said He would provide for His people. Even the desert that was once a wasteland is now blooming with abundant vegetation and food to partake of.

I am overwhelmed as I see the very words that the Lord wrote in the Bible coming to pass and realize that I am seeing and experiencing fulfilled prophecy every single day. It makes me raise my hands and thank the Lord for His Promised Word in Deuteronomy 26:9, "He brought us to this place and gave us this land, a land flowing with milk and honey..."

I pray that as you read each story and try the recipes, you will feel like you are right here in my kitchen in the Galilee, and we will sit down, break bread together, and enjoy the abundance of the Lord's fulfilled Word to His people Israel!

GIFT OF HOSPITALITY

So often we overlook the Gift of Hospitality. 1 Peter 4:9-11 says, "Be hospitable to one another without grumbling. As each one has received a gift, minister it to one another, as good stewards of the manifold grace of God." What exactly is the "Gift of Hospitality"? A good definition is, "The friendly reception of welcoming and treating guests or strangers in a warm, friendly, generous way. A thing given willingly to someone without payment; a present."

The word "gift" in Hebrew is "matahna." The verb is "natan," which means "give." It can be read from right to left, and also from left to right, which means "giving" can be both physical and spiritual.

The word "hospitality" in Hebrew is "ehrooach." The word "meal" in Hebrew is "ahroohah." The root of "ahroohah" is the same root of "ehrooach," meaning the meal and hospitality are connected!

Many women have said to me, "But I do not live in a big, beautiful house!" And I gently say back to them, "Neither did Abraham and Sarah, but they gave what they had to the three strangers." Genesis 18:1-8 is hospitality in action! Abraham greeted them with honor, water to wash their feet, and a place to rest. He brought bread to refresh them and had cakes and a young calf prepared for them to partake of. Now, that is the "Gift of Hospitality!"

If I do not have flowers on hand or cannot just go out and buy some, I go into my yard in the Galilee and literally pick "flowers" that are weeds and put them in little vases down the center of my table.

Almost every guest will say to me, "Oh, I need to do this, too!" There are so many plants that the Lord has provided for us to enjoy that bring warmth and a loving touch to any table. Even twigs of an herb can add an aroma of pure delight. I try to be as creative as I can with what I have in my house. It turns out to be so much fun to challenge myself.

Simply put, the Gift of Hospitality is loving, respecting, and honoring those who enter your dwelling place. Again, as 1 Peter 4:9 says, "Be hospitable to one another without grumbling." Every guest who enters your home will know if you have prepared everything with love and if you are happy to have them in your home, to serve them and to make them feel comfortable.

One time, some IDF soldiers who were stationed nearby because of the war, needed places to take showers. Noam and I among those who were happy to host them in our home. We greeted them with a huge welcome and let them know by our words how honored we were to have them. When they came in, I wanted them to smell the freshly baked chocolate chip cookies that were set out on the table, arranged with beautiful paper napkins and a pitcher of fresh lemon water with a sprig of mint floating on top. Every candle in the house was lit, and I laid out soft towels with new bars of soap and wrapped pieces of chocolate on top! They were so overwhelmed and thanked us a thousand times. And, of course, we prayed for them and sent them off with hugs and the rest of the cookies and told them that if they were ever in the Galilee, they were welcome to come and stay the night with us, and I would make them a beautiful breakfast in the morning with my freshly baked scones and lemon curd!

It's the simple things that are saturated with love that make the difference. When they see your love, they are not interested if your house is old or new, if the napkins are paper or cloth, or if the candles are expensive or from the dollar store.

There are so many examples of the "Gift of Hospitality" in the Bible. I encourage you to search them out and do your own study on them. I believe you will say, "Lord, I desire this gift to serve others with Your love and to make them feel safe and comfortable," and as I say, "Lord fill our home with Your Presence!"

TABLE OF FELLOWSHIP

I do believe that we all need to have a heart for the "Table of Fellowship" for family, friends, brothers and sisters in the Lord, and for new people we meet along the way, to share the love of Yeshua. The table of fellowship is a place of connection, love, forgiveness, conversation, closeness, and intimacy you just cannot get in a restaurant setting.

The word "fellowship" in Hebrew is "yedidoot," but the first four letters in the word

"yedidoot" are the word "yadeed," which means "friend." And in that word "friend" is the word "yad," which means "hand," and it is repeated twice, which means "hand to hand." How beautiful is that!

The biggest tables of fellowship that I know of were the ones that were spread out for the Jewish people and others in the Galilee over 2,000 years ago. One time, Yeshua Himself provided a meal for 5,000 men plus the women and children, and another time for 4,000 men plus the women and children. It was not a gourmet meal, but just consisted of bread and dried fish. Now, THAT is a "Table of Fellowship" and should encourage all of us to open our doors and welcome people to share at our own Table of Fellowship.

Because the setting of the Bible is in the Middle East, and with Yeshua specifically in Israel, there are Middle Eastern ways that we in the West will not understand until we understand the Word through Hebrew eyes, and then we will see deep into the root of the Olive Tree.

For example, when Peter went back to his occupation of fishing after he denied Yeshua three times, his thoughts and emotions, I am sure, were tormented every day as the memories of his words floated and darted against his conscience. You know the story in John 21, where Peter is in his boat and he hears a voice asking them if they had caught any fish, and of course Peter responded and said, "No." The voice then said, "Cast the net on the right side of the boat, and you will find some."

So, Peter and the other disciples that were with him did exactly that, and they caught such an overload of fish that they were not able to draw in the net! When Peter realized it was the Lord, he put on his outer garment and plunged into the sea. And, low and behold, as he arrived on the shore, he saw that Yeshua had built a small fire and had fish and bread ready for them to eat.

In the middle east, when someone offers you a meal and you accept it, whatever differences there had been between you are put aside and peace between you is restored. It is truly a table of forgiveness and of forgetting those things that are behind and moving toward the new. One of my favorite scriptures is Revelation 3:20, "Behold, I stand at the door and knock. If anyone hears My voice and open the door, I will come in to him and dine with him, and he with me." This is the perfect picture of reconciliation, Oh, how wonderful the Lord is to present to us "His Table of Fellowship," and now it is our turn to do the same, whether it is forgiveness, renewing friendships, or just wonderful fellowship to share with one another.

But the one that overwhelms me above them all is the "Marriage Supper of the Lamb." The Lord has invited us to the most incredible "Table of Fellowship" with Him for eternity! So let us now, in our temporary setting, open our doors to those who are looking for fellowship and invite them to our own "Table of Fellowship!"

MY JOURNEY TO FIND THE SPICES OF ISRAEL

Ok, I admit I don't speak Hebrew very well after living here on and off for over 12 years, but I have an incredible Israeli husband who does, and that is the mercy of the Lord to me. My husband always says to me, "Beloved, don't be so hard on yourself. You have the language of the heart, and that is the most important language." MELT DOWN!

I cannot begin to tell you how many spice shops I have been to in Israel, and just when I think I've seen all the spices there could possibly be, I always find something new. I cannot get enough of the amazing fragrances and beauty of them all. Each one tells its own story, and now I am telling you my story about the ones that have caught my attention and sparked my vivid imagination and creativity.

I am always trying to figure out the ingredients of the different spice mixes, and I ask the shop owners to tell me. The problem is that one shop gives me one answer, and I think, "Okay, now I know!" And then I go to the next spice shop, and they tell me something completely different. THAT'S ISRAEL!

Do I know the scientific, chemical reaction of one spice touching another? NO! Do I even understand why to use baking powder versus baking soda? NO! But out of determined curiosity, I am ready to try anything and everything.

So, to get to the truth of it, who am I? Someone who never had a garlic clove in her house in the States and who now puts garlic in everything. Someone who had every kind of electrical kitchen gadget you can buy at Walmart, but who now has to search the entire city for a normal coffee pot. Someone who has never watched a cooking channel in her life and who now, if there is ever free time, is glued to the TV, ready to try a new recipe on anyone who enters our house.

My greatest joy is to have people sit at our table of fellowship, whether it be morning, noon, or evening, to enjoy a meal that was made with love. Like Noam always says to our guests, "May your stomachs be full when you leave, but may your spirits be filled to overflowing!"

Even to this day, friends who have known me forever say, "Is this really you? What has happened to you? You have become a new person!" Yes, it is me, and yes, I am a new person every day in the Lord, and He has truly spiced up my life, living in Israel. Remember, it's time to spice up your life, too, and enjoy all the flavor that the Lord has given to us. To the Spice of Life, L'Chaim!!

SPICES IN ISRAEL

ZA'ATAR – I personally believe it is the #1 spice!

Caraway Seeds

Black pepper

Cloves

Anise Seeds – licorice flavor

Coriander

Paprika (so many flavors)

Cardamom

Nutmeg

Cumin

Cloves

Cinnamon

Oregano

Thyme

Marjoram

Sumac

Sesame seeds

Salt

HEBREW IN THE KITCHEN

Flour – ke'mach

Baking powder – aveqat afiah

Baking soda – sodah laafiah

White Sugar – sukar lavon

Brown sugar – sukar chum

To Knead - lalush

Mixing - irbuv

Salt – milakh

Pepper – pilpel

Butter – khem'a

Milk - khalav

Water - mayim

Oil – shemen

Cheese - gvina

Bread -lekhem

Vanilla – vanilla (lol)

Apron - sinar

Oven - taynur

Refrigerator – m'qarer

Stove - taynur

Fruit – pheri

Apple – tapu'ach

Orange – tapuz

Banana – banana (lol)

Grapes – anavim

Vegetable – yerek

Onion – beatzal

Garlic – shum

Cucumber – melafefon

Tomato – agvaniya

Green Pepper – pilpel yarok

Lettuce – haza

Carrot – gezer

ZA'ATAR

Story Time: To live in Israel, you must have in your kitchen the spice, za'atar. We have enjoyed many wonderful foods with the spice of za'atar sprinkled on them. Use your imagination and sprinkle it on anything that seems to fit with your palate. You will impress your guests with the Middle Eastern spice called za'atar.

I remember having to ask a grocery store clerk in the States for the spice za'atar, and the look on her face was of total puzzlement. I totally understood because before I moved to Israel, I had no idea, either, but NOW za'atar is a must on everything. You may be able to find it in a health food store or a Middle Eastern market. ENJOY!

INGREDIENTS:

½ cup sumac

2 Tbsp thyme

2 Tbsp roasted sesame seeds

2 Tbsp marjoram

2 Tbsp oregano

1 Tbsp coarse salt

1 tsp minced basil

DIRECTIONS:

1. Grind sesame seeds in food processor.
2. Add the remaining ingredients.
3. Store in airtight container.

INCREDIBLE OLIVE OIL

How can you write a cookbook in Israel and not write about "olive oil," which is the most precious liquid gold in your kitchen? Olive oil represents so many things in the Bible: The Holy Spirit, joy, abundance, and peace.

Let's start at the beginning, when Noah waited to see if the land was ready to receive his family again after the flood. He sent out a dove and the dove returned with an olive branch in its mouth. The land was ready to produce again the way the Lord had planned.

For centuries, olive oil was used for cooking, making soaps and cosmetics, anointing kings and the sick, lighting lamps in homes, and especially for keeping the lamp in the temple lit continually.

Every Israeli home has fresh olive oil for every purpose you can think of. It is abundant, and you can find it everywhere. Our favorite way to buy it is to stop on the side of the road in the Galilee and buy a huge plastic bottle of olive oil from a local merchant who produced it from olive trees passed down to him from generation to generation. It is exhilarating, to say the least! I never understood the precious gift that the Lord gave His people when He filled the land with olive trees, and now I can partake of it every day of my life in my home in the Galilee.

There are so many ways to use olive oil in recipes, but our favorite is making pita bread and dipping it into a small dish of olive oil topped with za'atar. Use your wonderful imagination and have fun, as olive oil in your kitchen is a prized possession!

Psalm 104:15 says, "…And wine that makes glad the heart of man, OIL to make his face shine, and bread which strengthens man's heart."

enjoy!

SMOOTHIES

MID-DAY COFFEE/COCOA SMOOTHIE

STORY TIME: Here in Israel, there are coffee shops everywhere, with people sitting inside or outside, in hot or cold weather. You think Seattle is known for coffee? Well, I am here to say that in the Middle East, Israel has great coffee and Israelis love to have fellowship over anything that has coffee in it. So here is a great version of a smoothie that will bring your tastebuds to life! Enjoy!

INGREDIENTS:

1 banana

2 Tbsp. date syrup (or substitute honey)

½ cup unsweetened almond or oat milk

1 Tbsp. unsweetened cocoa powder

1 cup very strong brewed or instant coffee(cold)

¼ teaspoon cardamom (a secret Ingredient!)

¼ teaspoon cinnamon

2+ cups Ice

DIRECTIONS:

1. Put all ingredients into a blender and blend well.
2. Sprinkle a little extra cocoa powder on top of this delectable smoothie.

BOKER TOV (GOOD MORNING) SPINACH/AVOCADO SMOOTHIE

STORY TIME: To look out my kitchen window in the Galilee and see beautiful avocados hanging from the tree during its season is such a gift. The avocados are so perfect and there is not one brown spot on the outside nor on the inside of the fruit. Avocado trees can be seen in the very northern part of Israel and all the way down to the southern tip of Israel. This smoothie is the perfect accompaniment for a special Shabbat morning brunch, or for breakfast any time. "Then God said, 'I give you every seed-bearing plant on the face of the whole earth and every tree that has fruit with seed in it. They will be yours for food.'" Genesis 1:29. Enjoy!

INGREDIENTS:

3 cups spinach or 8 frozen spinach cubes

1 avocado, pitted, peeled, and cubed

1 cup almond milk
(sweetened or unsweetened, to your taste)

1 medium banana, peeled

1 medium/large cucumber

1 Granny Smith apple, cored/cubed

3 dates

1 Tbsp honey

½ tsp lemon juice or freshly squeezed lemon juice

Ice to your liking

DIRECTIONS:

1. Add spinach, avocado, almond milk, and banana in blender until just combined.
2. Add cubed apple, cucumber, dates, honey, lemon juice, and blend until smooth.
3. Add ice to the amount you prefer.

Just a note:

This amount makes up to 6 small glasses. To add a special touch, garnish it with a few spinach leaves or take a couple of mint leaves to put on top. I personally love adding edible pansies as a beautiful way to impress your guests at the Shabbat brunch table.

COHENS' LIMONANA

STORY TIME: There was a favorite coffee shop in Jerusalem that I would go to as often as I could when I was visiting Israel before I came to live here. The Lord so directed me to this coffee shop close to the Mahane Yehudah Market, and to this day, I cherish the friendship that the Lord gave me with the owner. Sweet memories of Noah always flood over me with such joy, as we would often sit and share about our lives together. There was something so special about my friend Noah, and there was one thing that he could do like no other café owner. Usually, you give a waiter your desired drink order and get what you ordered, but not with Noah. HE would decide what I should be drinking for that day. Many times, he would bring me a limonana, even if I ordered a latte. And it was the BEST limonana ever! So, when I make our limonana, Noah always comes to my heart. By the way, the drink is called "limonana" because it is made with lemon and mint ("limon" and "nana" in Hebrew). Enjoy!

INGREDIENTS:

1 cup freshly squeezed lemons

1 large handful of mint leaves and its stems

¼ - ½ cup of sugar

½ - ¾ cup of cold water

3 cups of ice

DIRECTIONS:

1. Place all ingredients in blender and blend until smooth.
2. Garnish glass with a twig of mint and a slice of lemon.
3. An added tip: freeze the leftover limonana in ice cube trays and add the cubes to a soda water to enjoy another cold drink for the summer. If you do not mind a little bit of lemon liqueur, freeze small ice cubes of the liqueur and put into either cold drink.

SPREADS

APPLE AND DATE SPREAD

STORY TIME: When you drive during the season that produces heavy-laden apple trees in Israel, it is overwhelming to the eyes. The beauty of the red varieties of apples seems like a watercolor sent down from heaven. Then you drive by the date palm trees that gently sway to the breeze; it is like the trees are dancing to the sound of heavenly music that only they can hear. The blending of these two flavors together is truly a treat. Enjoy!

INGREDIENTS:

3 small, sweet apples cut up in chunks

1 cup sweet red wine

10 dates, pitted

½ cup raisins

Pinch of salt

1 cup chopped walnuts

2 Tbsp hawaij cookie spice or cinnamon

DIRECTIONS:

1. Put chopped apples in the food processor.
2. Add dates, pinch of salt, hawaij cookie spice or cinnamon, red wine and raisins, and process until smooth.
3. Add chopped walnuts after removing the mixture from the food processor.
4. Serve in a small serving dish and save the rest in the refrigerator.

AVOCADO AND SPINACH SPREAD

STORY TIME: Our house in the Galilee has an avocado tree, and we were both so happy when we saw it in the yard. Did you know that avocados are actually a fruit? Avocados here in Israel are used in so many recipes that it is just fun to experiment with them. This spread can be an accompaniment to crackers, pita bread, or any bread. Enjoy!

INGREDIENTS:

2 cups fresh spinach

1 ½ cups diced avocado

½ cup sour cream

¼ cup chopped red onion

1 Tbsp fresh lime juice
  (if you do not have lime juice, substitute with lemon juice)

1 garlic clove

½ tsp salt

¼ tsp pepper

1 tsp flaked hot pepper or a hot spice of
  your choice

DIRECTIONS:

1. Process spinach, avocado, sour cream, red onion, lime juice, garlic, salt, pepper and
   hot pepper spice in a food processor until smooth.

TAHINA EGGPLANT SPREAD

STORY TIME: I love going out to eat with my husband in any restaurant in Israel. You are barely in the door, not even in your chair yet, and they are already setting all the fine spreads before you with pita bread for dipping. It is the best. This is such an easy spread to make and partake of with your friends and family. Enjoy!

INGREDIENTS:

1 large eggplant

3 garlic cloves, finely chopped

2 Tbsp tahina

1 Tbsp sour cream

½ tsp lemon juice

1 medium onion, chopped fine

2 Tbsp parsley, chopped

½ tsp salt

1 tsp paprika to garnish

DIRECTIONS:

1. Preheat oven to 400 degrees F.
2. Wash and poke eggplant with fork.
3. Place it on a baking sheet and bake for 50 minutes or until soft.
4. Scoop out eggplant and place it in food processor.
5. Add garlic, tahina, sour cream, lemon juice, onion, parsley, and salt, and process just seconds until combined.
6. Serve in a serving bowl with paprika sprinkled on top.

HUMMUS

STORY TIME: I must admit that when I go into a local restaurant here in Israel, I am always surprised to see a young couple order only a saucer of hummus with pita on the side - that's it. And they love it! Now I have become one of them - maybe not just hummus and pita, but with a grilled chicken breast and a typical Israeli salad on the side. Yummy! Enjoy!

INGREDIENTS:

2 15-oz cans chickpeas (garbanzos)

2 Tbsp olive oil

1 Tbsp lemon juice

½ cup tahina

3 garlic cloves, peeled and crushed

½ tsp salt

Garnish: pour 1 Tbsp olive oil into center, sprinkle za'atar and paprika on top

DIRECTIONS:

1. Place all ingredients into a food processor (not a blender) and blend until very smooth.
2. Add garnish.

DEBORAH'S DELIGHTFUL LEMON CURD

STORY TIME: The story I am about to tell you is one of my most emotional experiences while living outside of Jerusalem in the Judean Hills. We lived in an apartment on the 3rd floor, and across the way was another apartment whose outside area faced ours. I had noticed that my neighbors had a beautiful lemon tree, heavy with fruit, in a very large container on their merpeset (Hebrew for balcony). From my kitchen window, I saw this fruit every day, but they never once picked a lemon. We were invited to come over to their place one night for dessert and I asked, "Why don't you pick your beautiful lemons?" Here is the heartwarming story the gentleman told me: They were born and raised in Russia, and as Jews, they longed to come home (Aliyah) to Israel, but they did not have the funds to do it and had to save money for their hearts' desire.

He then told me that only the wealthy people in Russia had lemon trees. He said that one day when the Lord would make a way for them to do Aliyah, he would buy a lemon tree but never pick its fruit. He would just relish the reality that they were rich in every way because they now lived here in the land that God gave to His people. He rejoiced every day when he looked at his own lemon tree with beautiful lemons hanging on it. So, you can imagine what it is like now for me to live in a house in the Galilee where our landlord planted two lemon trees. It seems like it was just for me so I can always look out my window and rejoice that the Lord brought me, also, into this land, living with the most amazing husband walking beside me! Enjoy!

INGREDIENTS:

4 large eggs

1 cup sugar

½ cup lemon juice

¼ cup limoncello (optional)

¼ cup butter

1 Tbsp lemon zest

DIRECTIONS:

1. Grate lemon until you have 1 tbsp zest.
2. Whisk 4 large eggs.
3. In double boiler on medium-high heat place eggs, sugar, lemon juice, limoncello, butter, and lemon zest, stirring continually until the mixture coats the back of a wooden spoon.
4. Let cool for about 15 minutes and pour into a delightfully designed jar and serve guests with a smile on your face. They will rave over it. Enjoy!

BREADS

EASY SHABBAT CHALLAH

STORY TIME: I can remember the first time I ever made challah bread for Shabbat dinner and was so proud of myself, knowing that I did it before the Lord. My revelation of Shabbat changed my life forevermore. Just knowing that Jesus (Yeshua) said, "I am the Lord of the Sabbath," led me right into the Ancient Paths towards Mt. Zion. "This is what the Lord says: 'Stand at the crossroads and look; ask for the ancient paths, ask where the good way is, and walk in it, and you will find rest for your souls.'" Jeremiah 6:16. This recipe is not hard, but my word of encouragement to you is "do it unto the Lord and enjoy every step of the way as you present it to your guests at the Table of Shabbat." Enjoy!

INGREDIENTS:

¼ cup light brown sugar

¼ cup vegetable oil

½ tsp salt

1 cup hot water

1 package dry yeast

¼ cup lukewarm water

½ tsp sugar

3 eggs

4-5 cups flour

1 Tbsp poppy seeds

1 Tbsp sesame seeds

1 tsp coarse sea salt

1 tsp dried garlic (optional)

1 tsp dried onion (optional)

DIRECTIONS:

1. Combine brown sugar, oil, and salt in a large bowl.
2. Pour in 1 cup hot water and stir to blend.
3. In separate bowl, stir yeast into ¼ cup lukewarm water with ½ tsp sugar.
4. Beat 2 eggs. Add eggs and yeast to first mixture: blend well.
5. Gradually add flour to make a soft dough.
6. Knead until smooth and elastic and fingers pull out cleanly from dough.
7. Cover and let rise for one hour, when doubled, punch down.
8. Divide into three portions and roll each piece into a long thin roll.
9. Braid the 3 pieces together.
10. Place on a sprayed non-stick cookie sheet and let rise again.
11. Beat 3rd egg and brush over the top. Sprinkle with poppy seeds, sesame seeds and coarse sea salt. Dried garlic and dried onions optional.
12. Bake at 350 degrees F for about 40 minutes or until done.

GALILEE

FLATBREAD

STORY TIME: I have eaten so many kinds of flatbread here in Israel because the different ways of making it is passed down from generation to generation and each family has their own unique version of it. This is a funny story because my son Kevin was in Hawaii, and he showed me a picture of what he had for dinner, and it looked marvelous. I told him it was flatbread served with a beautiful feta salad on top, and it inspired me at that moment to make it for guests when they came for lunch or dinner, especially in the hot summer months here. Enjoy!

INGREDIENTS:

2 cups flour (white or whole wheat)

½ tsp baking soda

1 tsp baking powder

1 tsp garlic powder

1 ¼ cup of 2% milk

2 Tbsp olive oil

Garnish

olive oil

Himalayan salt

Za'atar

DIRECTIONS:

1. Combine flour, baking soda, baking powder, salt, garlic power and za'atar and whisk together.
2. Add milk slowly while kneading all together.
3. Cover and let stand for 10 minutes.
4. Put 2 Tbsp olive oil in frying pan and bring to a nice heat.
5. While the frying pan is heating up, flour your hands and take a small portion of the bread, pull and form into a flat thin layer. Place into frying pan and fry for about 2 minutes on each side. Add more oil to the pan as needed.
6. To garnish brush oil on top of bread and sprinkle with Himalayan pink salt and za'atar.
7. Experiment with your own techniques but you can use this wonderful flatbread in so many ways in your meals.

SWEET CHEESE BOUREKAS

STORY TIME: There is nothing like enjoying a sweet cheese boureka at your favorite coffee shop in Israel. Noam and I love to go on fun outings to coffee shops just to sit and talk and meet people. We have four "favorite" coffee shops in a nearby Galilee town that we love, and honestly, we have become family with the employees and the local patrons alike. Greetings of "Shalom!" bring huge smiles to our faces. Many times, we have met people for the first time at these shops and, of course, invited them to our Shabbat table on a Friday night or to my delightful Shabbat Brunch on a Saturday. Many of them have become close friends. Just like our friends, there are all kinds of bourekas, sweet and savory, but I have to say my favorites are the sweet ones! Enjoy!

INGREDIENTS:

1 package frozen puff pastry (take out the night before and put in refrigerator)

1 cup cream cheese   ½ cup of flour

1/3 cup sugar   ½ cup melted butter

3 eggs   sesame/poppy seeds

DIRECTIONS:

1. Preheat oven to 350 degrees F.
2. In mixing bowl whip together cream cheese, sugar, and 2 eggs.
3. Mix in flour.
4. In a separate bowl beat the third egg for your egg wash.
5. Cut puff pastry into 4" squares, brush egg wash on the edges to be able to close
   the edges.
6. Place a good amount of your cheese mixture in the square and then diagonally close
   the edges.
7. Take a fork and press into edges to secure the open ends.
8. Brush melted butter over top of bourekas and garnish with poppy seeds or sesame
   seeds or a touch of sprinkled sugar.
9. Bake for 25-30 minutes or until golden brown.

BREAKFAST

JUDEAN HILLS SPINACH QUICHE

STORY TIME: When we lived in the Judean Hills outside of Jerusalem, it was so beautiful and more laid back than downtown Jerusalem. Making a Shabbat brunch is, to this day, a wonderful time in the kitchen. Why? Because Noam is right beside me chopping all the ingredients! When you visit Israel, make sure you also drive through Ein Kerem up to the hills and take in the beauty of the landscape. Enjoy!

INGREDIENTS:

1 cup cottage cheese

1 cup sour cream

6-8 eggs

½ tsp pepper

½ tsp salt

2 cups shredded cheddar cheese

2 cups frozen chopped spinach
  thawed and squeezed dry

2 cups frozen broccoli
  thawed and well drained

1 small onion, chopped

1 small yellow pepper, chopped

1 small red pepper, chopped

4 garlic cloves, minced

8 mushrooms, sliced

pinch of za'atar spice

sweet paprika (garnish)

DIRECTIONS:

1. Sautee onion, yellow pepper, red pepper, and garlic in a skillet with non-stick cooking spray.
2. Add broccoli and spinach.
3. Add mushrooms and finish sautéing.
4. Remove when vegetables are soft, and onions are a beautiful golden color.
5. In a separate large bowl whisk together eggs.
6. Add cottage cheese, 1 ¾ cup cheddar cheese, sour cream, pepper, and salt.
7. Bake at 350 degrees F and check the quiche at 45 minutes, and if knife comes out clean, it is done.
8. Top with ¼ cup of cheddar cheese, sprinkle za'atar and sweet paprika to decorate.

CAPERNAUM BROCCOLI QUICHE

STORY TIME: One of the quickest brunch recipes I make in Israel is quiche. They are so easy, especially if you do not do a pie crust. I prefer not to have a pie crust because it just adds more calories. My advice, as I have done here in the land, is to experiment with different ingredients and spices. I love the creativity and the freedom of creating new recipes here in Israel. Many of our precious friends are "taste testers" who have happily agreed to taste my recipes anytime I call them. Enjoy!

INGREDIENTS:

6 eggs

1 cup milk or heavy cream

1 Tbsp garlic flakes

3 cups broccoli, chopped into
   small pieces

¼ tsp cayenne spice

1 cup cheddar cheese

½ tsp salt

DIRECTIONS:

1. In large bowl, whisk together eggs, milk, garlic, salt, and cayenne.
2. Stir in cheese.
3. Add broccoli to egg mixture and pour into pan that has been sprayed with nonstick cooking spray.
4. Bake at 350 degrees F for around 40-45 minutes until knife comes out clean.
5. Just a little garnish of paprika is a wonderful addition to your beautiful, easy quiche.

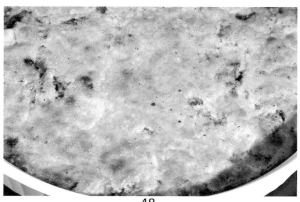

SHAKSHUKA MORNING

STORY TIME: This is such a Middle Eastern dish, and everyone loves it whether it is for breakfast, lunch, or dinner. When you are invited to a friend's house for Shakshuka, it is always a surprise to see what spices and ingredients they have chosen to make their unique version of it. But, no matter the ingredients, it is always called "Shakshuka!" The word Shakshuka actually comes from the Arabic word that means "mix!" Well, I am going to say "mix it up" for your friends and family, and when you present this dish, watch their amazement as they witness your talents in the kitchen! Enjoy!

INGREDIENTS:

¼ cup olive oil

1 green pepper, chopped

1 yellow pepper, chopped

1 large yellow onion, chopped

3 green onions (scallion) thinly sliced

4 garlic cloves, crushed

1 tsp cumin

½ tsp cayenne pepper

1 can 28oz whole peeled tomatoes/liquid

6 eggs, room temperature

1 cup chunked feta cheese

salt and pepper to taste

DIRECTIONS:

1. Sauté peppers and onions in olive oil stirring constantly over medium heat.
2. Add garlic, cumin, cayenne pepper. Continue stirring for about 4 minutes or until garlic is soft.
3. Mash whole tomatoes with masher and add to skillet.
4. Simmer 12 to 15 minutes over medium heat or until slightly thickened.
5. Crack eggs into tomato sauce, cover skillet, and cook about 15 minutes.
6. Sprinkle with chunked feta cheese.
7. Season with salt and pepper.
8. Serve immediately.

MY ISRAELI SCONES

STORY TIME: I love having tea with friends here in Israel with fancy teacups, scones, and my delightful lemon curd, and they love it too. I always place beautiful napkins on the table with a vase full of our gorgeous bougainvillea that grows abundantly in the Galilee. You can have fun with various kinds of flour with this recipe and you must decide how much cream to put in the recipe according to your liking. I love using heavy cream and wheat flour with this recipe, but I have made it with a variety of flours. So many times in the kitchen the Holy Spirit reminds me of a scripture while I am baking, and here is one to meditate on: Deuteronomy 8: 7-8, "For the Lord your God is bringing you into a good land, a land of brooks of water, of fountains and springs, that flow out of valleys and hills; a land of wheat and barley, of vines and fig trees and pomegranates, a land of olive oil and honey...." Always remember to have fun, and when your guests realize you made the scones, they will love them even more! Enjoy!

INGREDIENTS:

2 cups whole wheat or white flour

1/3 cups white sugar

1 Tbsp baking powder

½ tsp salt

6 Tbsp cold unsalted butter, cubed

1 ½ cups heavy cream

1 large egg

1 tsp vanilla

DIRECTIONS:

1. Preheat oven to 400 degrees F.
2. Combine flour, sugar, baking powder, and salt together in medium sized mixing bowl.
3. Add cold cubed butter to flour mixture and use a pastry cutter to make into pea size pebbles.
4. In a separate bowl whisk together heavy cream, egg, and vanilla.
5. Add wet ingredients to the dry mixture, stir until just combined.
6. Place mixture onto floured surface; make into about a 6" round ball and use a rolling pin to gently flatten top.
7. Cut into 8 equal triangles.
8. You may put into refrigerator for 15 minutes to just get a chill on the dough, but I usually do not do this because I am always in a hurry!
9. Brush the top with some heavy cream and sprinkle with sugar.
10. Place on a greased baking sheet, and bake approximately 18 to 20 minutes until the bottom of the scones are a beautiful golden brown.

SALADS

KINNERET CHICKPEA SALAD

STORY TIME: We had a friend's friend come and stay with us in the Galilee for a few days, and this is a recipe I came up with for the "Duke from France." I think even aristocrats will rave over this delicious salad that was created in my kitchen. The Land of Promise is flowing with fruits, vegetables, and of course, the Biblical seven species of the Land: figs, dates, grapes, pomegranates, wheat, barley and olives! Chickpeas are a staple in Israel, and I love being creative with them and so will you. So, when you come to Israel, you must try everything, and your taste buds will come alive. Enjoy!

INGREDIENTS:

1 can chickpeas (garbanzo beans) drained

1 can corn, drained

4 Tbsp olive oil

1 tsp minced garlic

1 Tbsp minced onion

1 purple onion, sliced

2 Tbsp fresh lemon juice

¼ cup chopped cilantro

¼ cup fresh mint

salt and pepper to taste

DIRECTIONS:

1. In a large bowl toss all ingredients together and season with salt and pepper.

FETA
PASTA
SALAD

STORY TIME: When the Feast of Shavuot (Pentecost) comes, this is the perfect salad to make with wonderful feta cheese. Israelis love feta cheese, or I should say, Israelis love any type of cheese, especially if you get it from one of the many cheese farms here in the Galilee. It is a must to visit one, and so much fun to taste all of their beautiful cheeses served with an amazing view of the Land of Naphtali and Zebulon in the North. Enjoy!

INGREDIENTS:

1 package (16oz) shell pasta or any plump pasta

2 cucumbers, chopped in large chunks

20 cherry tomatoes, cut in half

1 cup feta cheese, crumbled

½ cup mint leaves, cut

5 Tbsp olive oil

4 Tbsp lemon juice

3 tsp Dijon mustard or your favorite

1 red pepper

5 green onions, chopped

¼ cup minced onions

2 Tbsp powdered garlic

½ cup sliced black olives.

salt and pepper to taste

garnish with paprika

DIRECTIONS:

1. Whisk together olive oil, lemon juice, Dijon mustard, salt, and pepper.
2. Add minced onions and powdered garlic.
3. Boil pasta according to package directions, drain.
4. In large bowl add chopped cucumbers, tomatoes, mint leaves, green onions, black olives, and red pepper.
5. Add pasta and feta and mix.
6. Add whisked wet ingredients and mix. If needed, add more olive oil or other ingredients to make the most delicious salad for any occasion.

TANGY FENNEL SALAD

STORY TIME: I went to a friend's house, and she made me a salad, and in this salad was a vegetable I had never tasted before. She said it was fennel, and I fell in love with the taste. Just remember, for me living in Israel, everything became exciting to try.

This is such a refreshing dish to serve before the main course. I never knew how wonderful the fennel vegetable is to incorporate into salads. Try it, and if you do not know what it looks like, it looks like a hand with 5 fingers! Enjoy!

INGREDIENTS:

4 mandarin oranges

1 fresh fennel, finely sliced

1 Tbsp chopped dill

3 Tbsp olive oil

1 Tbsp butter

4 Tbsp pine nuts

½ cup pomegranate seeds

½ cup dried cranberries

DIRECTIONS:

1. Peel & segment mandarin oranges. If the segments are too large, slice in half.
2. Combine the oranges, fennel, and dill in a bowl, toss with olive oil.
3. Place in refrigerator to cool.
4. Sauté pine nuts in 1 Tbsp of butter in a sauté pan on low heat until brown, before serving.
5. When ready to serve, sprinkle the sauteed pine nuts, pomegranates, and dried cranberries over individual serving plates.

REFRESHING TABOULEH SALAD

STORY TIME: I remember a friend made this salad for a luncheon on my patio in the Judean Hills. We had at least 27 people and they all enjoyed it. Do not be shy; try new ingredients until you can make it your own. Again, this beautiful green shade of salad reminds me of the scripture: "The Lord is my Shepherd; I shall not want. He makes me to lie down in green pastures, He leads me beside the still waters." Psalm 23:1-2. Enjoy!

INGREDIENTS:

1 cup bulgur wheat

6 cherry tomatoes, cut in half

3 cups fresh parsley, chopped fine

3 cups mint leaves, chopped fine

6 green onions, chopped fine

1 cup olive oil

3 lemons juiced

salt and pepper to taste

DIRECTIONS:

1. Soak bulgur in hot water for 30 minutes.
2. Drain and squeeze with your hands until all moisture is removed.
3. Add parsley, onions, and mint leaves to bulgur.
4. Mix olive oil and lemon juice and pour over bulgur salad.
5. Salt and pepper to taste.
6. Top with sliced cherry tomatoes.

SIDE

DISHES

DRUZE ROASTED CAULIFLOWER

STORY TIME: Noam and I love going to quaint little restaurants or coffee shops in Israel. Meeting new people, who wind up becoming dear friends, has happened repeatedly, and of course, we invite them to our home for Shabbat dinner or Shabbat lunch. This wonderful story is over roasted cauliflower! We were at a Druze restaurant, and Noam and I did not know what to get, so we were looking around at what other people had ordered. I spotted a beautiful dish with something displayed on it, but I could not detect what it was. So, I got up and went over to the couple and asked what it was. They spoke English, and told me it was a special type of baked cauliflower that the chef loved to serve at this restaurant. Then, they said, "We cannot eat the whole cauliflower, so when we have had enough, we will bring it to your table to try." In that moment, we made new friends, Ofra and Alon; we have been to their house, and they have been to ours, all because of a beautiful cauliflower dish at a Druze restaurant in the Galilee. This is Israel, or maybe just me being ME! Enjoy!

INGREDIENTS:

1/3 cup extra virgin olive oil

1 tsp minced parsley

1 tsp thyme

1 tsp za'atar

4 crushed garlic cloves

1 tsp sea salt, coarse

½ tsp pepper

¼ cup parmesan cheese, grated

DIRECTIONS:

1. Preheat oven to 400 degrees F.
2. In a small bowl, mix oil, parsley, thyme, za'atar, garlic, salt, and pepper together.
3. Wash cauliflower and cut leaves off but do not separate the cauliflower, keep it intact.
4. Turn the cauliflower upside down and spread some of the mixture into the grooves of the cauliflower.
5. Turn it right side up and spread the rest of the mixture over the top and press into the cauliflower.
6. Cover and bake for 30 minutes, then uncover the cauliflower and bake for an additional 30 - 45 minutes until fork goes smoothly into cauliflower.
7. Bake an additional 10 minutes after sprinkling the parmesan cheese over the top, for a beautiful garnish that will enhance the taste.

OPTIONAL: After it is removed from the oven, you may drizzle tahini over the top and let it run down the sides. Wonderful option to enjoy.

GALILEE STUFFED MUSHROOMS

STORY TIME: Here in Israel mushrooms are used almost daily. In Western Galilee there is a large farm that supplies much of the mushrooms that Israelis consume. Since living here, I love experimenting with stuffing mushrooms with a variety of ingredients. When you add Tahini as a drizzle over the mushrooms, it brings your taste buds right to Israel. Enjoy!

INGREDIENTS:

12 large mushrooms, stems removed

1-1 ½ cups of ground beef

3 Tbsp butter

1 small onion, chopped & diced

5 garlic cloves, minced

1-1 ½ cups shredded cheddar cheese

½ cup cilantro, chopped fine

tahini

DIRECTIONS:

1. Wash and pat dry mushrooms and place on a baking sheet sprayed with non-stick cooking spray.
2. Place 3 Tbsp butter in skillet, add diced onion and garlic, sauté about 3 minutes.
3. Add hamburger to the onion and garlic, cook until hamburger is done.
4. Remove hamburger, onion, and garlic from skillet and let cool a bit.
5. Add a small dollop of butter in each mushroom and place hamburger mixture in each mushroom until almost overflowing.
6. Add as much shredded cheddar cheese as you can on top.
7. Place in a 325 degree F oven until the cheese is melted.
8. Remove from the oven and add more cheese on top and garnish with chopped cilantro.
9. Now drizzle with quality tahini and serve warm.

Optional: Ground turkey would also be a wonderful option instead of hamburger.

FRIED EGGPLANT

STORY TIME: The first time I ever saw a fried eggplant in Israel, it was not an appetizing sight! You must understand I came from Northwest Washington where I had not even touched an eggplant before, let alone eaten one. Now that I have eaten this delectable food, I am smitten, for sure. Remember to garnish the dish with a spread that they can also enjoy with each bite of fried eggplant. Enjoy!

INGREDIENTS:

1 large eggplant, peeled & sliced thin

½ tsp pepper

2 eggs, beaten

½ tsp coarse salt

½ cup whole milk

2 Tbsp za'atar (or thyme)

1 cup white flour

2 Tbsp canola oil, use more if needed.

DIRECTIONS:

1. Wash and peel large eggplant and slice thin, about ¼" thickness.
2. Combine eggs and milk in bowl.
3. In a separate bowl, mix together flour, pepper, salt, and za'atar.
4. Dip eggplant slices into egg mixture and then dip both sides into flour mixture.
5. Place in frying pan with oil on medium heat.
6. Cook 2-3 minutes on both sides until eggplant is soft.
7. Remove and place on paper towels to get rid of excess oil.
8. Serve immediately.

MAIN

COURSES

FRAGRANT PUMPKIN SOUP

STORY TIME:

When we lived outside of Jerusalem in the Judean Hills, we loved to stop by a little market owned by Arabs who we had come to love. Every time we would walk into the little market, I would try to teach one of the sons a new English word. It was a delightful time as we got to know each one of the family members. It was pumpkin season, and when I walked into their market, I saw the biggest pumpkin I had ever seen in my life. I saw that they had a huge knife with which they had carved out pieces for those who came to purchase the deep orange chunks of delightful pumpkin. The young man that I had been teaching English noticed my amazement at the enormous pumpkin and carved out a huge piece for me and etched a heart in it. We miss this family and their delightful market, but now whenever we drive to Jerusalem, we try to stop by and greet one another with love. On a cold winter day – yes, readers, Israel can be quite cold in the winter, with wind and rain coming from every direction – it takes a steaming bowl of soup to warm you up. With a wonderful muffin beside your soup, you will have a delightful winter day in Israel. Enjoy!

INGREDIENTS:

1 cup onions, chopped	1 Tbsp brown sugar
4 garlic cloves, crushed	¼ tsp nutmeg
3 Tbsp butter	¼ tsp pepper
2 cups canned pumpkin	3 ½ cups chicken broth
2 cups cooked yams (mashed)	half-and-half for consistency (if needed)
1 tsp salt	za'atar to garnish

DIRECTIONS:

1. Sauté onions and garlic in butter in medium-sized soup pan on stove.
2. Add pumpkin and mashed cooked yams.
3. Add salt, sugar, nutmeg, pepper, and brown sugar to mixture.
4. Add chicken broth and heat until it just begins to boil.
5. Pour in half-and-half for desired consistency to your taste. Blend with stick blender.
6. Garnish with za'atar.

DESERT HONEY CHICKEN

STORY TIME: Living in Israel is a gift from above. In this small strip of land, the Lord has put everything that brings you pleasure to enjoy. If you want snow, it is Mt. Hermon. If you want to raft down a river, it is the Jordan River. If you want to swim, it is the Sea of Galilee. If you want to float and not sink, go to the Dead Sea. If you want to feel the waves against your body, it is the Mediterranean Sea. If you want to experience what Abraham and Sarah lived like, go to the desert. Most people have no idea that the desert gives you everything you need. The Hebrew word for desert is "debar," which means "to speak." In the quietness of the desert is where you will hear the Lord speak to you without the noise of life that most of us live with. Isaiah 30:15; "...thus said the Lord God, the Holy One of Israel, 'In returning and rest you shall be saved; in quietness and confidence shall be your strength.'" So, as you eat the Desert Honey Chicken, quiet yourself and listen. Enjoy!

INGREDIENTS:

½ cup extra virgin olive oil

2 tsp ground cumin

2 cloves of garlic, crushed

2 Tbsp date honey

1 tsp Himalayan salt

2 Tbsp cabernet sauvignon wine

6 boneless chicken breasts

DIRECTIONS:

1. Mix oil, wine, cumin, garlic, date honey, and salt together in small bowl.
2. Place chicken in an oiled shallow baking dish and pour the marinade over the top.
3. Place in refrigerator for 4 hours to marinate before baking, and spoon or brush marinade from dish over the chicken several times while in refrigerator.
4. Bake at 375 degrees F for 45 – 50 minutes or until golden brown and fork enters easily in the chicken pieces. Use a meat thermometer to make sure done.
5. Serve immediately.

CHICKEN CUMIN KABOBS

STORY TIME: Okay, I am going to let you in on a secret; Israelis barbecue anywhere and at any time of the day! One time Noam and I were driving home really late at night around Midnight, and there on the side of the road was a picnic table with three young men barbecuing away as if it were daytime. Israelis love kabobs, especially if they have meat on them. Marinating your meat in Israel is common, or sometimes they mix spices and rub it into the chicken. We enjoy marinating the chicken in the ingredients below, and especially adding the cumin to spice it up. Enjoy!

INGREDIENTS:

6 chicken breasts, cubed

1 cup olive oil

1 Tbsp lemon juice

3 garlic cloves, minced

½ cup parsley, chopped

1 tsp cumin

1 Tbsp date honey

salt and pepper to taste

DIRECTIONS:

1. In large bowl, mix together olive oil, lemon juice, garlic, parsley, cumin and date honey.
2. Place chicken cubes in mixture and marinate for at least 3 hours in the refrigerator.
3. Skewer the chicken, salt and pepper to taste.
4. Grill chicken until tender and cooked through.

JEZREEL VALLEY BROCCOLI CASSEROLE

STORY TIME: The Feast of Shavuot (Pentecost) is one of my favorite feasts. We love having people at our table of fellowship and serving them delicious dairy products. This feast is known for its dairy products. But this recipe is about broccoli, which is normally grown in the fertile farmland of the Jezreel Valley where wheat, corn, cotton, and beautiful sunflowers are also grown. And, of course, where herds of sheep and cattle graze, enjoying every bite. It is also the time of the barley harvest and the romantic story of Boaz and Ruth, giving of the Torah, and, of course, the giving of the Holy Spirit to the 120 believers who waited in Jerusalem for The Promise to come. This recipe was a hit at our table, and we know you will love it, too. Enjoy!

P.S. This feast is such a reminder of the season that Noam and I met; the Jewish man meets the non-Jewish woman in the field of Israel!

INGREDIENTS:

2 packages of powdered mushroom soup, made into a condensed consistency (here in Israel you cannot find a can of condensed mushroom soup). But in the USA, use 1 can of condensed cream of mushroom soup.

4 chicken breasts, cooked & cubed

1 cup mayonnaise

2 eggs, beaten

½ cup onions, chopped

4 garlic cloves, minced

1 medium bag of frozen chopped broccoli

1 small red pepper, diced

3 ½ cups finely grated carrots

2 cups of cheddar cheese, shredded

salt and pepper to taste

paprika and za'atar to garnish

DIRECTIONS:

1. On medium heat in saucepan, mix together mushroom soup, mayonnaise, egg, onions, red pepper, and garlic.
2. Sprinkle with salt and pepper.
3. In large bowl, put broccoli and carrots, and stir in mushroom soup mixture.
4. Add the cooked chicken, and 1 ½ cups cheddar cheese and mix well.
5. Spread into a greased baking dish.
6. Sprinkle remaining ½ cup of cheddar cheese over top.
7. Then sprinkle with paprika and za'atar.
8. Bake at 350 degrees F in your choice of 9x13 glass baking dish.
9. Bake for 45 minutes or until done. Serves six people.

BAKED CUMIN SALMON

STORY TIME: When you walk through any open market in Israel, the aroma of spices fills your nose with absolute delight. The spice, cumin, is extremely popular in Israel, and I have become a fan, too. I had dinner with my Noam in a hotel in Jerusalem and tasted the best salmon ever. Of course, I went to the chef and asked him, "What is the secret?" And he said, "Cumin!" Enjoy!

INGREDIENTS:

6 salmon fillets

¼ cup olive oil

2 Tbsp ground cumin

1 Tbsp mustard seeds

2 Tbsp dijon mustard

1 Tbsp honey

pink Himalayan salt and pepper to taste

DIRECTIONS:

1. Preheat oven to 400 degrees F. Spread olive oil in 9x13 inch baking dish.
3. Rinse salmon fillets and dry; spread olive oil on both sides and lay in baking dish.
4. Mix together Dijon mustard, honey, mustard seeds, and ground cumin; pour over salmon fillets.
5. Salt and pepper to taste.
6. Bake uncovered until desired doneness or until salmon flakes with fork.

DESSERTS

MALABI
WITH A
DEBORAH'S TWIST

STORY TIME: In most Arab restaurants, you will find this extraordinary dessert that is so well known in the Middle East, and of course, in Israel. At first, the taste might surprise you, but with every bite, you will find yourself wanting more. One night, we had invited a beautiful Armenian Christian sister to our Shabbat Table. I was so nervous because she, of course, grew up with this dessert, but I was determined to make my own version of it. Well, she loved it!!! And I know you will, too, and you can surprise your dinner guests with this amazing delight. Enjoy!

INGREDIENTS:

2 cups whole milk (in Israel it is 3% milk)

1/3 cup of sugar

5 Tbsp cornstarch

½ cup water

¼ cup heavy whipping cream

1 tsp rosewater

DIRECTIONS FOR MALABI BASE:

1. In a small saucepan, whisk together milk and sugar.
   Stir over medium heat until it starts to boil.
2. In a small bowl, mix cornstarch and water until smooth.
3. Add cornstarch mixture into milk and sugar mixture in saucepan.
4. Bring it to a boil and stir until thickened for approximately 2 minutes.
5. Remove from heat.
6. Stir in cream and rose water and cool for about 20 minutes, stirring occasionally to keep it smooth.
7. Transfer to clear glass dessert dishes.
8. Place plastic wrap over pudding and refrigerate until cold. I prefer overnight.

See the next page for syrup recipe:

POMEGRANATE SYRUP

INGREDIENTS:

½ cup sugar

½ cup pomegranate juice

1 tsp rose water

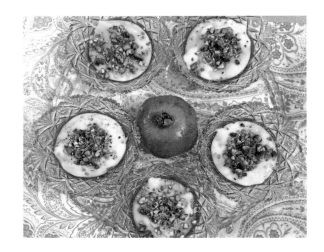

DIRECTIONS FOR SYRUP

1. In a small saucepan, combine sugar, pomegranate juice, and rose water. Cook and stir over medium heat until sugar is dissolved and it becomes a smooth syrup.
2. You may want to add more pomegranate juice as you are stirring, to adjust the consistency of the syrup to your own liking.
3. Remove from heat and cool completely before you spoon the syrup over the pudding.
4. A must is to sprinkle chopped pistachios and then some whole pistachios on top of the syrup.
5. You may opt to add grated white chocolate over the pudding and then add some finely-chopped unsweetened cranberries to decorate.
6. Or you may choose to sprinkle pistachios with flaked coconut. Be creative!

ABU GOSH POMEGRANATE BARS

STORY TIME: When we were remodeling our apartment outside of Jerusalem, we had to find a place to rent, and we choose to live in Abu Gosh, an Arab city that has never fought against Israel. I learned so many wonderful tricks of the trade from my beautiful Arab neighbors. Not only from my neighbors, but also from the lush nature around our apartment that was constantly giving me ingredients. And one of those ingredients was the "Pomegranate." It is a beautiful fruit that has a crown upon its top and comes forth during the Feast of Rosh Hashanah, the New Year. It is such a symbol to us Believers because we all know who wears the crown, Yeshua Ha Mashiach. Enjoy!

INGREDIENTS:

½ cup sugar

1 tsp cinnamon

1 cup pomegranate seeds

1 cup raisins

1 cup grated carrots

3 Tbsp butter

1 cup apple juice

½ cup water

2 eggs

2 cups flour

2 tsp baking soda

½ tsp salt

1 cup chopped walnuts

DIRECTIONS:

1. Preheat oven to 325 degrees F.
2. In a small saucepan, combine sugar, cinnamon, pomegranate seeds, raisins, carrots, butter, apple juice, and water.
3. Bring to a boil, reduce heat and simmer for 7 minutes, stirring as needed.
4. Pour mixture into a large bowl and cool in refrigerator for 15 minutes.
5. After the mixture has cooled for 15 minutes, mix in the eggs.
6. In a separate bowl combine the flour, baking soda, and salt, then add to the cooled carrot mixture.
7. Mix well and stir in the walnuts.
8. Pour into a greased 9x13 inch baking pan.
9. Bake for 30 - 35 minutes until the toothpick comes out clean.

MEDITERRANEAN COOKIES

STORY TIME: This is such a fun recipe for me since I discovered the Arabic spices here in the land. If you cannot find the specific spices in your local grocery store, please check out the spices in a health food store or a Mediterranean specialty store and ask specifically for Middle Eastern Spices. Enjoy!

INGREDIENTS:

½ cup butter

½ cup sugar

½ cup light brown sugar

2 eggs

2 tsp vanilla

2 ¼ cups flour

1 tsp "ras el hanout" spice

1 tsp salt

1 tsp baking soda

1 cup coconut

1 cup dried cranberries

1 cup pistachio nuts (coarsely chopped)

DIRECTIONS:

1. Cream butter and sugars together, then add eggs and vanilla.
2. Add remaining dry ingredients but do not over mix.
3. Add coconut, cranberries, and pistachio nuts, refrigerate for 30 minutes.
4. Drop by spoonful on sprayed cookie sheet and flatten only slightly.
5. Bake at 350 degrees F. for 10 – 12 minutes.

YANSON (ANISE) COOKIES

STORY TIME: I made these incredible cookies after purchasing the anise seeds at a spice shop today. I was determined to put the delicious smell of the anise seeds into a cookie recipe. This is what I came up with and I think it is one of the most elegant, beautiful, delicious cookies I have ever eaten. My husband, Noam, is eating these tonight for a Shabbat dessert. He loves them! Enjoy!

INGREDIENTS:

2 cups white flour

1 tsp baking powder

3 Tbsp anise seeds

½ tsp salt

1 tsp cinnamon

2 eggs, room temperature

1 tsp vanilla extract

½ cup butter, softened

2 Tbsp whipping cream or half-and-half

¾ cup sugar

TOPPING:

½ cup powdered sugar

1 tsp vanilla extract

2 Tbsp whipping cream or half-and-half

1/3 cup pistachio nuts in food processor

DIRECTIONS:

1. Preheat oven to 350 degrees F.
2. Mix butter and sugar together, then add eggs.
3. Beat mixture on low speed until fluffy, then add vanilla extract and whipping cream.
4. In a large bowl combine flour, baking powder, anise seeds, salt and cinnamon.
5. Add flour mixture into egg mixture.
6. Lightly flour hands and roll into 1" balls and place on sprayed cookie sheet. Pat down slightly.
7. Bake 10-12 minutes or until golden brown.
8. Topping – Stir powdered sugar, vanilla and whipping cream together.
9. Dip slightly cooled cookies into topping and then dip into crushed pistachio nuts.

GOLAN HEIGHTS LAVENDER COOKIES

STORY TIME: A friend told Noam about a lavender farm in the Golan Heights called Azizo in Kibbutz Kanaf. The view is breathtaking as you drive up the side of the Golan Heights! As you approach the entrance to the farm and take in the view of the lavender fields, you know this place is a hidden treasure. The owners are a delightful couple who greeted us with a smile and offered us iced lavender tea. The gift shop has amazing products, and the aroma of lavender brings such a calmness over you. Now let's investigate where lavender is mentioned in the Bible. John 12:3 says, "Then Mary took a pound of very costly oil of spikenard, anointed the feet of Yeshua, and wiped His feet with her hair. And the house was filled with fragrance of the oil." Spikenard is actually lavender, and that is why this farm is so special!

They have a wonderful cookie recipe made with dried lavender, but you know me, I have to create my own recipe for you to try. Be creative with your ingredients, but at the same time, ask the Lord in your heart, "What can I give you, Lord? It is my praise and worship to You! Receive this as a beautiful aroma that comes through me to You, Lord!" Or, "It is my absolute devotion to You, Lord; may it all become a beautiful fragrance to You!" Enjoy!

INGREDIENTS:

2 cups flour

1 tsp baking powder

Pinch of salt

1 Tbsp plus 1 tsp dried lavender

¾ cup butter, softened

½ cup sugar

zest of 1 lemon

1 egg

3 Tbsp lemon juice

DIRECTIONS:

1. In a mixing bowl whisk flour, baking powder, pinch of salt and dried lavender together.
2. In separate bowl beat together butter, sugar, and lemon zest, then add the egg and lemon juice. Beat well until light and fluffy.
3. Now combine dry ingredients and wet ingredients together and mix by hand.
4. Refrigerate for at least 30 minutes.
5. Roll into 1" balls, flatten a little bit and place on parchment paper on cookie sheet.
6. Bake 350 degrees F for 10-12 minutes until bottoms of cookies are golden brown.

ICING FOR CENTER OF COOKIE INGREDIENTS

1 cup powdered sugar
1 tbsp butter

1 tbsp lemon juice
lime zest (optional)

Mix the icing ingredients together to your preferred consistency, and for a tangy twist, sprinkle lime zest on the frosting.

NATHANAEL APPLESAUCE FIG CAKE

STORY TIME: I must admit this is truly my favorite fig cake of all time. Figs have such a history in Israel, and even King Solomon recognized the significance of the fig tree. "And Judah and Israel dwelt safely, each man under his vine and his fig tree, from Dan as far as Beersheba, all the days of Solomon." 1 Kings 4: 25.

Eating a fresh fig off of a tree in Israel is like a burst of joy in your mouth. So, you can imagine how Nathaniel felt when he met Yeshua for the first time, and Yeshua knew who he was. "'How do you know me?' Nathanael asked. Yeshua answered, 'I saw you while you were still under the fig tree before Philip called you.'" John 1:48. Enjoy!

INGREDIENTS:

2 cups all-purpose flour

¾ cup sugar

1 tsp salt

1 tsp cinnamon

½ tsp nutmeg

½ tsp cloves

2 tsp baking soda

2 tsp baking power

1 cup raisins

1 cup chopped walnuts

1 cup diced dried figs

2 eggs

½ cup butter, melted

1 ¾ cup applesauce

¼ cup cappuccino yogurt

DIRECTIONS:

1. Preheat oven to 350 degrees F.
2. Sift (or whisk) together the dry ingredients in a mixing bowl.
3. In a separate bowl, mix melted butter, applesauce, and cappuccino yogurt. Beat at low speed until well blended. Add eggs and beat on low speed until well blended again.
4. Add raisins, chopped walnuts, and diced dried figs; mix well.
5. Pour batter into a greased and floured 9-inch square pan.
6. Bake for 40 minutes or until a toothpick comes out clean.
7. Cool and spread with cream cheese frosting.

PASSOVER CHARMING CAKE

STORY TIME: This is such a delightful cake for the Feast of Passover (Pesach), especially if you are trying not to use flour during this time. Whether that is the reason or not, I love the ingredients and the flavor of this cake. During the Feast of Passover here in Israel, most people will remove yeast from their homes and eat matzah crackers. I am so thankful that the Lord has removed the yeast (sin) from our lives and has replaced it with His righteousness. But when we go to someone's house for Passover, we are always aware of how each household honors this Feast, and we abide by their ways. Enjoy!

INGREDIENTS:

4 eggs (small)

1 ½ cups vegetable oil

¾ cup milk caramel liqueur (or syrup)

1 ½ cups sugar

3 cups matzo meal

1 cup cornstarch

2 tsp ground cinnamon

10 apples – peeled, cored, and sliced

¾ cup brown sugar

2 tsp ground cinnamon

1 tsp hawaij spice (substitute nutmeg)

½ cup chopped walnuts

DIRECTIONS:

1. Preheat oven to 350 degrees F.
2. Grease a large 10" or 11" springform pan.
3. Combine eggs, oil, milk caramel liqueur or syrup, and white sugar in a bowl and mix on medium speed. Stir in matzo meal, corn starch and 2 tsp cinnamon.
4. In a separate bowl, toss apples with brown sugar, 2 tsp cinnamon, and 1 tsp hawaij.
5. Spread half of the dough into the bottom of the prepared pan and pour the apples on top of it. Place the remaining dough over the apples, gently spreading to reach the sides of the pan.
6. Sprinkle the top with some brown sugar and chopped walnuts.
7. Bake for 45 minutes or until a toothpick comes out clean.

LEMON TREE CAKE

STORY TIME: This is a wonderful cake that you will make repeatedly for your family and for the guests who come to your home for a visit. I have made this cake more than any other cake because it is the easiest cake to make at the last moment. There are times that friends will unexpectedly call and say, "Hey, we would love to come over in a couple of hours, is that OK with you?" I never fret anymore because of this very elegant little cake. With this cake, you can add a creative toppings to each cake you make. I like to use raspberries crowned with a dollop of whipped cream. I also try to add a sprig of mint as I slice each piece, and it just adds the finishing touch to it that guests will appreciate. Enjoy!

INGREDIENTS:

2 cups flour

2 tsp baking powder

2/3 cup sugar

4 eggs

Syrup:

4 Tbsp powdered sugar (or you
   (can determine the amount)
3 Tbsp lemon juice

2/3 cup sour cream

5 Tbsp lemon juice

2 Tbsp lemon zest

2/3 cup vegetable oil

DIRECTIONS:

1. Sift flour and baking powder together in medium bowl.
2. In small bowl beat eggs until fluffy and then add sugar and beat. Now add to the egg and sugar mixture the sour cream, lemon rind, lemon juice and oil and beat until all is combined.
3. Pour wet ingredients into dry ingredients and mix well until all is combined.
4. Pour mixture into a prepared springform pan and I like the 8" pan.
5. Bake at 350 degrees for 50 minutes or less, test with toothpick. Look for a light golden color around edges of pan.

6. For the syrup, mix the powdered sugar and lemon juice together in a small pan, stirring until it just begins to boil. Again, if you want to make more syrup to pour over your cake, please do!
7. When the cake comes out of the oven, poke several holes on the top with a large fork and pour the syrup over the surface. Let the cake cool before removing it from the springform pan.

Just some fun suggestions to top this lovely cake:

1. As I said earlier, you can make a raspberry mixture to top each piece and add some whipped cream with a sprig of mint.
2. Or just dust top of cake with powdered sugar.
3. Or you can use cream cheese frosting on top and sides if you want!

BE CREATIVE AND HAVE FUN!

PROMISED LAND
CHEESECAKE

STORY TIME: Cheesecake seems to be a staple at any restaurant here in Israel. Of course, on the Feast of Shavuot (Pentecost), it is a must to have a dairy dessert. I have observed that when I make this cheesecake, everyone wants this recipe because it is simple and easy. One Shabbat night we had a beautiful couple for dinner. He was from New York and she was from Colombia, and I had made my cheesecake. Suddenly, I thought, "Oh no, he is from the land of New York Cheesecake! Why am I serving my cheesecake to him?" Guess what? He loved my cheesecake and had a second piece! My recipe was created in the Promised Land and, of course, it is delicious. Enjoy!

INGREDIENTS:

Crust:

1 ½ cups crushed graham crackers or any plain sugar cookies

1/3 cup of butter, melted

Filling:

2 (8 ounce) packages of cream cheese
(Israeli cream cheese is the best!)

3/4 cup white sugar

1 tsp vanilla or any flavored liqueur

1 ½ cups sour cream

3 eggs, room temperature

DIRECTIONS:

1. Preheat oven to 350 degrees F. Grease an 8 or 9-inch springform pan.
2. Blend cookies until they are fine. Mix in melted butter and press into bottom of pan.
3. Bake crust for 8 minutes.
4. In large bowl mix cream cheese with eggs on low speed until smooth.
5. Beat in sugar and vanilla.

6. Mix in sour cream with hand mixer on low just until blended.

7. Pour into prepared crust.

8. Bake in oven for 30 minutes. Turn off oven and let sit in oven for another hour.

9. Chill in refrigerator until ready to serve.

OPTIONAL TOPPING:

I love to add a dollop of heated berries with a touch of sugar and place it on top and let it run down the sides of the cheesecake.

And of course, I add a sprig of mint from my herb garden to bring this cheesecake to its full flavor and beauty!

MATCHA TEA CAKE VIA JAPAN

STORY TIME: You say, "What does matcha tea have to do with Israel?" Well, here is the answer: Noam lived in Japan for 20 years, trying to find "The Way of Life," and ended up coming back to Israel and finding "The Way" through Yeshua. He loves matcha, so I decided to try to make this cake when I saw how beautiful it could look with the deep green color of the matcha. I need to tell you, I worked on this recipe a few times and found that organic matcha tea powder is the best, and I found it at a health food store. So glad Noam made his way back to Israel where he became a born-again Jewish man who was born in the City of Jerusalem! PLUS, "HE IS MY HUSBAND!" You will love Matcha tea cake. Enjoy!

INGREDIENTS:

4 medium eggs

½ cup sugar

1 tsp vanilla

½ cup vegetable oil

½ cup vanilla yogurt

1 ½ cups cake flour

1 tsp baking powder

2 Tbsp organic matcha powder

DIRECTIONS:

1. In large bowl, beat eggs first, then add sugar, vanilla and oil, and beat until light and fluffy.
2. Now gently fold in yogurt until combined.
3. In separate bowl, whisk flour, baking powder, and matcha powder until combined.
4. Gently fold flour mixture into wet mixture.
5. Spray cake pan with non-stick butter spray.
6. Heat oven to 350 degrees F.
7. Bake in oven for around 35 minutes or until toothpick comes out clean.

CREAM CHEESE FROSTING (Optional):

I love the taste of this smooth topping. I use 8 ounces of cream cheese and add powdered sugar to taste. Beat together. It is a simple, but wonderful topping for the matcha cake. I would also suggest that whipped cream with a bit of sugar added is just as delightful. You can, of course, add a mint leaf to garnish!

INCREDIBLE CARROT CAKE

STORY TIME: I must admit, this carrot cake recipe is so much fun to do. I will have another carrot cake recipe in my next cookbook just because I love carrots and so do Israelis. This fun recipe is a reminder to me to always be thankful for the abundance that springs upward from the Promised Land of plenty! This cake is perfect for guests when you want to show off your culinary skills. They will ask you for the recipe. Enjoy!

INGREDIENTS:

4 eggs, room temperature

2 cups all-purpose flour

1 ½ cups sugar

2 tsp baking powder

½ tsp baking soda

¼ tsp salt

5 cups finely shredded carrots

½ cup cooking oil

¼ cup orange juice

2 tsp peeled fresh ginger, grated

1 cup walnuts, chopped finely

Add frosting of your choice

Optional: edible pansies for decoration

DIRECTIONS:

1. Preheat oven to 350 degrees F. Grease two 9-inch round cake pans and line bottom with parchment paper.
2. In a large bowl combine flour, sugar, baking powder, baking soda and salt.
3. In a smaller bowl combine lightly beaten eggs, carrots, oil, orange juice and ginger.
4. Stir egg mixture into flour mixture until combined.
5. Stir in nuts.
6. Spread batter into pans, bake for 30-35 minutes or until a toothpick comes out clean.
7. Cool in pans on wire rack for 15 minutes, then remove from pans and cool thoroughly on racks.
8. Place one layer on serving plate and spread enough frosting to edges.
9. Stack the second layer flat side down and spread the remaining frosting.

MT. ARBEL CHOCOLATE CAKE

STORY TIME: Well, this is a fun story. When I first started coming to Israel, of course, I wanted to buy souvenir gifts for family and friends. I was offered a sample of this special Israeli chocolate by my tour guide, but he did not tell me it had tiny pieces of popping candy in it that would literally pop in your mouth. Oh my, did I have a surprised look on my face when they began to pop in my mouth and kept popping! But trust me, I am not asking you to get this chocolate. Still, it would be a fun idea to see if it would pop in your guest's mouth if you added it to the recipe. I am going to have to try it sometime! As a decoration to this special chocolate cake, I like to add three pieces of white chocolate leaning on one another on top. Israelis love chocolate and since I have moved here, I have come to appreciate it, too. A piece of chocolate any time of the day is fine with me! Enjoy!

PS: It has to be over 72% cocoa to meet Noam's healthy standard, so I do not feel guilty when I partake!

INGREDIENTS:

2 ½ cups all-purpose flour

1 cup white sugar

¾ cup cocoa powder

2 tsp baking soda

1 tsp baking powder

1 cup buttermilk
  (or add 1 Tbsp lemon juice or
   to 1 cup milk to make buttermilk)

½ cup vegetable oil

3 eggs, at room temperature

1 tsp vanilla extract

1 teaspoon salt

¾ cup freshly brewed hot coffee

2 cubes of dark chocolate

1 Tbsp chocolate liqueur or dark chocolate syrup

DIRECTIONS:

1. Preheat oven to 350 degrees F.
2. Whisk flour, sugar, cocoa powder, baking soda, baking powder and salt together in medium bowl.
3. In a small bowl, break up chocolate and pour hot coffee over it until melted.
4. In a large bowl, combine buttermilk, oil, eggs, vanilla, chocolate liqueur or dark chocolate syrup, and hot coffee mixture together and mix with hand mixer.
5. Slowly add dry ingredients to the wet ingredients with mixer on low speed.
6. Pour batter into sprayed cooking pan or lightly flour sides with spray oil and then add parchment paper to line bottoms of 2 9-inch round cake pans or 1 springform cake pan.
7. Bake 30-35 minutes or until toothpick comes out clean.
8. Cool cake pans for at least 15 minutes until cool to the touch.

FROSTING:

INGREDIENTS:

4 ounces dark baking chocolate (or
  60% cocoa chocolate bar)
1 stick of butter at room temperature

1 Tbsp chocolate liqueur or dark
  chocolate syrup
1 ½ to 2 cups sifted powdered sugar
1 Tbsp instant espresso coffee
  powder or instant coffee crystals
2 Tbsp buttermilk

DIRECTIONS:

1. Preheat oven to 350 degrees F.
2. Melt chocolate and butter together over heat-proof bowl set over a pan of simmering
  water.
3. Add chocolate liqueur, espresso coffee powder (or instant coffee is fine).
4. Add buttermilk, stir, and remove from heat.
5. Add powdered sugar and beat with hand beater to your desired consistency. If
  consistency is too thick, add a bit of half-and-half.
6. Spread on the bottom layer of cake and then on top layer and sides.

SUNSET GALILEE DESSERT

STORY TIME: Trust me, you will love this very Middle Eastern dessert that is served in most Druze or Arab restaurants here in Israel. I love meeting the chefs, and I always ask the waiter if the chef can come out so I can tell him (or her) how much we enjoyed their creative talents with food. At one of these restaurants, a wonderful chef came out and was so happy to meet us and to serve us, and, of course, wanted to know who we were. What an opening to share our lives with him! The waiter then told me the ingredients that he knew belonged in the dessert, but there were quite a few missing. So, here comes the adventurer that I am in my kitchen, and I just went for it. I served this dessert to an Arab Believer, and she loved it! So, enjoy, as we did, the beautiful dessert while sharing our testimonies of how we met our Redeemer, Yeshua! Enjoy!

INGREDIENTS:

Main Base:

1 cup semolina flour (fine)

1/3 cup sugar

2 Tbsp vanilla pudding mix

5 cups whole milk

1 ½ Tbsp rose water

Topping Over Base:

3 cups heavy cream

½ tsp rose water

½ cup powdered sugar

Syrup Topping:

1 cup sugar

2 cups water

A few drops rose water

Additional Toppings:

2 cups coarsely crushed pistachios

1 cup pomegranate seeds

DIRECTIONS:

1. In saucepan, add fine semolina, sugar, and pudding mix, and whisk together. Add milk and whisk on med/high heat. As it begins to thicken, lower to medium heat, and whisk continually until the mixture becomes pudding-like. Remove from burner and add rose water. Pour into 9" X 13" glass baking pan, cover with plastic wrap, and set on counter to cool for at least 25 minutes, and then refrigerate for no less than 1 hour, but preferably for at least 3 hours.

2. In a separate bowl, add heavy cream and beat on high speed, slowly adding the rose water and powdered sugar until the mixture forms a peak. Cover with plastic wrap and refrigerate until the main base has completely cooled in refrigerator.

3. Remove both the base and whipped cream mixture from the refrigerator and spread mixture over the base. Cover the dessert with crushed pistachios (and add more if you would like!) You will love it. Then sprinkle pomegranate seeds over the pistachios.

4. Cover with plastic wrap and return to refrigerator until ready to serve.

5. Place all the syrup topping ingredients in a saucepan over med/high heat until dissolved, then let completely cool.

6. Slowly dribble syrup over the dessert, or if you have small pitchers, fill some to place beside the dessert for each guest to decide how much they want.

DEBORAH'S TABLE SETTINGS

NOAM

Made in the USA
Columbia, SC
24 November 2024

46687606R00071